In its growth from tiny, fumbling and narrowly conceived beginnings in the early 19th century to the large, modern "multiversity" of today, Indiana University may stand as a prototype of the American state university.

Thomas D. Clark in *Indiana University (Vol. 1)*

Clock Tower, Student Building

INDIANA
UNIVERSITY

PHOTOGRAPHED BY BILL LUSTER

HARMONY HOUSE

PUBLISHERS LOUISVILLE

We wish to thank all the hard-working people of the Indiana
University Alumni Association for their help in the logistical
and pre-production phases of this book. Joan Curts, in particular,
was tremendously supportive and helpful during the entire course
of the project. Thanks also to John Hobson for his help in editing
and review. And, finally, thanks to the staff at the University
Archives for their help in researching the text for the book.

Photograph on page 85 courtesy of NCAA/ Host Communications.
The publisher and photographer wish to thank Patrick Limm, Chris
Usher, Tom Hirschfeld, Richard Schultz, Rogers Construction Co.
and Linda and Joseph Luster for their contributions to this book.

Executive Editors: William Butler and William Strode
Library of Congress Catalog Number: 86-082740
Hardcover International Standard Book Number: 0-916509-18-4
Printed in U.S.A. by Pinaire Lithographing Corp., Louisville, Kentucky
First Edition, October, 1987, from Harmony House Publishers-Louisville
P.O. Box 90, Prospect, Kentucky 40059 (502) 228-2010 / 228-4446
Copyright ©1987 Harmony House Publishers-Louisville
Photographs copyright © 1987 Bill Luster

Woodburn Hall

Overleaf: Showalter Fountain

9

Woodburn Hall

INTRODUCTION

By John McGreevey

"She's the pride of Indiana..." This book, filled with vibrant and eye-filling photographs of Indiana University, reminds all who turn its pages why our school — in its incomparable natural setting — with its wide-ranging architectural glories — because of the lives and accomplishments of its people — truly is "the pride of Indiana."

I left Indiana University in 1943 and emigrated from Hoosierdom the following year. But wherever work or whim carried me, an invariable has been the happy sense of connection I feel when I read of the University's widening world of influence, meet a fellow "exile," see or hear some small detail which carries me home once again to the friendly banks of the Jordan.

One of the more exotic such moments was in Chiang Mai, Thailand, when our young guide pointed out a lovely, flowering tree on the slopes of a ruined Buddhist shrine. My wife (an alumna of IU) and I laughed in delight and burst into spontaneous song: "Gloriana, FRANGIPANA!" We were halfway around the world but the Indiana University connection was still there.

How comforting it would have been over these many years to have had a book such as this with me. A kind of Family Album. Turn to almost any page at random, and you'll find yourself launched onto the gently flowing river of fond reminiscence. A single photograph reverberates into a hundred memory images.

Campus crowds. In the fieldhouse. One minute to play, the score tied. In front of the old Student Building. Linked arm-in-arm, exercising our right to protest. In the auditorium. Enthralled by Marian Anderson or Rudolph Serkin or Peter, Paul and Mary. Such shared excitements are treasured.

Another picture recalls solitary moments. Standing alone on the bare stage of the University Theatre, looking out into the empty auditorium. Or, in the Well House. A clear, cold, February night. The pure chiming of the clock on the Student Building tells me musically how late it is and how good to be alive and in this special place at this special time.

This book's possibilities are unlimited. If you bring to it, as I did, a sweet burden of nostalgia, you'll soon be happily lost in these familiar scenes. But, if you know little or nothing of Indiana University, I think you'll be intrigued by the world you find pictured. How easy to imagine yourself as part of this life!

Indiana University has many faces. Each of the hundreds of thousands of us who feel we know her see her just a little differently. And, of course, she is forever changing. The University preserves the best of yesterday, arms us to meet the challenges of today and prepares us for tomorrow.

Leaf through this book and you'll feel her strong attraction. Perhaps you'll be impelled, as I was, to revisit and renew old acquaintance in person.

Whether presented in these handsome photographs or seen again at first hand, the evidence is unmistakeable. From any and every point of view, our University was, is and always will be..." the PRIDE OF INDIANA!"

John W. McGreevey is a native Hoosier and IU alumnus. He is a writer whose scripts for such shows as "Roots" and "The Waltons," in addition to his numerous docudramas, have earned him an Emmy, a Peabody Award, three Christopher Awards and, in 1982, the Paddy Chayefsky Laurel, television writing's highest award. He received the University's Distinguished Alumni Service Award in 1973, and an Honorary Degree from the University in 1986.

A SELECTED IU CHRONOLOGY

1820 Legislative act adopted establishing a state seminary.

1822 Construction begins on Seminary building.

1824 Classes begin with an enrollment of ten men.

1828 By legislative act, State Seminary changes to Indiana College.

1829 Andrew Wylie named first president.

1830 First graduating class.

1836 First college building constructed in Seminary Square.

1838 Legislative act adopted changing Indiana College to Indiana University.

1842 School of Law established (suspended 1877-89; revived 1889).

1852 Legislative act adopted recognizing Indiana University as "The University of the State." Alfred Ryors named second president.

1853 William Mitchell Daily named third president.

1854 First college building destroyed by fire.

1855 Second college building constructed.

1859 Theophilus Wylie served six months as acting president. John Hiram Lathrop named fourth president.

1867 IU became one of the first state universities to admit women; the *Indiana Student* first published.

1874 Science Hall at Seminary Square completed.

1875 Lemuel Moss named sixth president.

1882 Charles Henry Gilbert became first to receive Ph.D. degree.

1883 Dunn's Woods, located east of downtown Bloomington, purchased from Moses F. Dunn; first intercollegiate game (baseball) played by an IU team.

1884 Wylie and Owen halls constructed on new campus (named University Park); Elisha Ballantine named acting president.

1885 David Starr Jordan (1885-91) named seventh president; Mitchell Hall (named Maxwell Hall until 1894) constructed on new campus.

1886 Men's football team started.

1890 Department of Physical Training for Women established, with gym in Wylie Hall; Library Hall (renamed Maxwell Hall in 1894) constructed.

1891 John Merle Coulter named eighth president; department of Physical Training for Men established, with gym in Owen Hall.

1892 Men's Gymnasium completed (razed in 1932).

1893 Joseph Swain named ninth president.

1894 Kirkwood Hall constructed; campus yearbook, *Arbutus*, first published.

1896 Second Men's Gymnasium constructed (renamed Assembly Hall in 1917; razed in 1938).

1898 Men's basketball team started.

1900 Kirkwood Observatory constructed; Wylie Hall partly destroyed by fire.

1902 William Lowe Bryan named tenth president; Science Hall constructed (renamed Ernest Hiram Lindley Hall in 1957).

1903 School of Medicine established.

1904 Graduate School established.

1906 Student Building constructed with funds from private subscriptions.

1907 Second Library Building completed.

1908 School of Education established; Theodore F. Rose Well House built with portals of the Second College Building.

1909 The Indiana Union for Men established.

1910 Biology Hall completed (renamed Swain Hall East in 1957).

1913 IU Alumni Association formed.

1914 Training School for Nurses established (renamed School of Nursing in 1956).

1917 Department of Military Science established.

1919 Indianapolis School of Medicine Building completed (renamed Charles P. Emerson Building in 1961).

1920 School of Commerce and Finance established (renamed School of Business Administration of 1933. School of Business in 1938).

1921 School of Music established.

1923 Commerce Building constructed (renamed Business Administration building in 1935, Social Science Building in 1941, William A. Rawles Hall in 1971).

1924 President's house completed; Washington Hall dormitory constructed (renamed South Hall in 1925, Ulysses H. Smith Hall in 1959).

1925 Women's Memorial Hall and Memorial Stadium (renamed Tenth Street Stadium in 1971) completed; School of

Dentistry established.

1928 Field House completed (renamed Wildermuth Intramural Center in 1971).

1931 Chemistry Building completed.

1932 Indiana University Memorial Union completed; men's wrestling and track teams won NCAA championships.

1934 School of Dentistry building completed on Medical Center campus at Indianapolis.

1936 Administration Building built (renamed Bryan Administration Building in 1957). School of Music Building, and Forest Hall (renamed Goodbody Hall in 1962) completed; IU Foundation established.

1937 School of Medicine Building at Bloomington completed (renamed Myers Hall in 1958).

1938 Herman B Wells named eleventh president; School of Business established; University School and Stores and Services Building (renamed Ernie Pyle Hall in 1954) completed; Clinical Building at Indianapolis completed; men's cross country team won NCAA championship.

1940 Alfred C. Kinsey Institute established; Beech (renamed Morrison Hall in 1942) and Sycamore halls added to Memorial and Goodbody halls to form Agnes E. Wells Quadrangle; North Hall (renamed Cravens Hall in 1959) and West Hall (renamed Edmondson Hall in 1959) added to men's residence complex (renamed Collins Living Learning Center in 1981); men's basketball and cross country teams won NCAA championships.

1941 IU Auditorium completed; one of world's first cyclotrons became operational at IU.

1942 Men's cross country team won NCAA championship.

1945 School of Health, Physical Education, and Recreation established.

1946 Dormitory unit completed (renamed John W. Ashton Center in 1980); several army buildings moved to campus for housing and classroom use.

1948 America's first degree-granting folklore program initated. Archives of Folk and Primitive Music founded (renamed Archives of Traditional Music in 1965); East Hall constructed (burned in 1968); Link Observatory donated by Goethe and Helen Link.

1949 Men's Quadrangle (renamed Joseph H. Wright Quadrangle in 1959) and University Apartments completed.

1950 IU Press established.

1952 Indiana Memorial Union admitted women for the first time.

1953 Men's basketball team won NCAA championship.

1955 Married housing unit completed (renamed Hepburn, Nutt, Bicknell, and Banta apartments in 1959); Jordan Hall of Biology and Smithwood Hall (renamed Daniel Read Hall in 1962) completed.

1956 School of Law Building completed; Beck Chapel constructed.

1957 Evermann Apartments completed.

1959 Ballantine Hall and Tower Quadrangle (renamed Nellie S. Teter Quadrangle in 1961) completed.

1960 Lilly Library completed; Seventeenth Street Football Stadium (renamed Indiana Memorial Stadium in 1971) and Athletic Field House completed; Married Student Housing complex (renamed Redbud Hill Apartments in 1961) erected.

1961 Graduate School of Business established; Woodlawn Dormitories (Morgan, Brown, Monroe, and Green halls) and Ruby C. Mason cooperative housing unit completed; Showalter Fountain completed.

1962 Elvis Jacob Stahr, Jr. named twelfth president; Herman B Wells named University Chancellor; Fine Arts Building, Geology Building, Campus View Apartments, and Residence Halls Administration Building completed.

1963 Psychology Building, Administrative Services Building, Radio and Television Building, and John W. Foster Quadrangle completed.

1964 Paul V. McNutt Quadrangle and new University School completed.

1965 Wendell L. Willkie Quadrangle and Tulip Tree House completed.

1966 Graduate Library School established (renamed School of Library and Information Science in 1980); School of Business Building, Student Health Center, and Forest and Herman T. Briscoe quadrangles completed.

1967 University acquired 245 acres on Monroe Reservoir to house Biological Research Station.

1968 Herman B Wells named interim president; Joseph Lee Sutton named thirteenth president; University's 150th Birthday Fund Drive publicly announced; Optometry Building and Speech and Hearing Building completed; Men's swimming team won NCAA championship; Football

team played in Rose Bowl.

1969 Third Library Building completed; Second Library Building burned (renamed Student Services in 1972 after repairs); Eigenmann Graduate Residence Center completed.

1970 Sesquicentennial celebrated; Credit Union Building completed; men's swimming team won NCAA championship.

1971 John W. Ryan named fourteenth president; Assembly Hall, Musical Arts Center, Black Archaeological Laboratory, Publications/Services Building completed; Metz Carillon donated by Arthur R. Metz Foundation. AIAW began first intercollegiate competition for IU women.

1972 Poplars Hotel purchased and renamed Poplars Research and Conference Center; second Library Building renovated as Student Services Building; Men's swimming team won NCAA championship.

1973 Black Culture Center Established; Men's swimming team won NCAA championship.

1974 School of Journalism established; Showalter House constructed by IU Foundation.

1975 School of Continuing Studies established; School of Optometry established.

1976 Men's basketball team won NCAA championship.

1977 New Geology Core Storage Building opened; Andrew Wylie House entered on National Register of Historic Places.

1978 Animal Care Building completed; *Breaking Away* filmed.

1979 Music Practice Building completed; football team won Holiday Bowl.

1980 Visitors Center opened; Old Crescent buildings placed on National Register of Historic Places.

1981 School of Journalism became systemwide school; School of Music students presented first performance by a university company at Metropolitan Opera House; Little 500/Soccer Stadium opened (renamed William S. Armstrong Stadium in 1982); IU Art Museum completed. Men's basketball team won NCAA championship.

1982 Leonard Bernstein in residence as first fellow of Institute for Advanced Study; Mathers Museum completed; American Studies Program in Yugoslavia established; women's tennis team won AIAW championship; men's soccer team won NCAA championship.

1983 Institutes established for American Theatre Studies, Molecular and Cellular Biology, and Materials Research; men's soccer team won NCAA championship.

1984 American Indian Studies Institute established.

1985 Campaign for Indiana began public fund drive; Owen and Wylie halls rededicated; Malaysia Project established; Transportation Center established.

1986 IU Foundation celebrated fiftieth anniversary; President John W. Ryan announced decision to leave office in 1987; Center for Entrepreneurship and Innovation established; Law School addition dedicated.

I hope our alumni will always insist upon retention of our precious islands of green and serenity — our most important physical asset, transcending even classrooms, libraries and laboratories in their ability to inspire students to dream long dreams of future usefulness and achievement — dreams that are an important part of undergraduate college experience.

Chancellor Herman B Wells

Overleaf: The Cyclotron

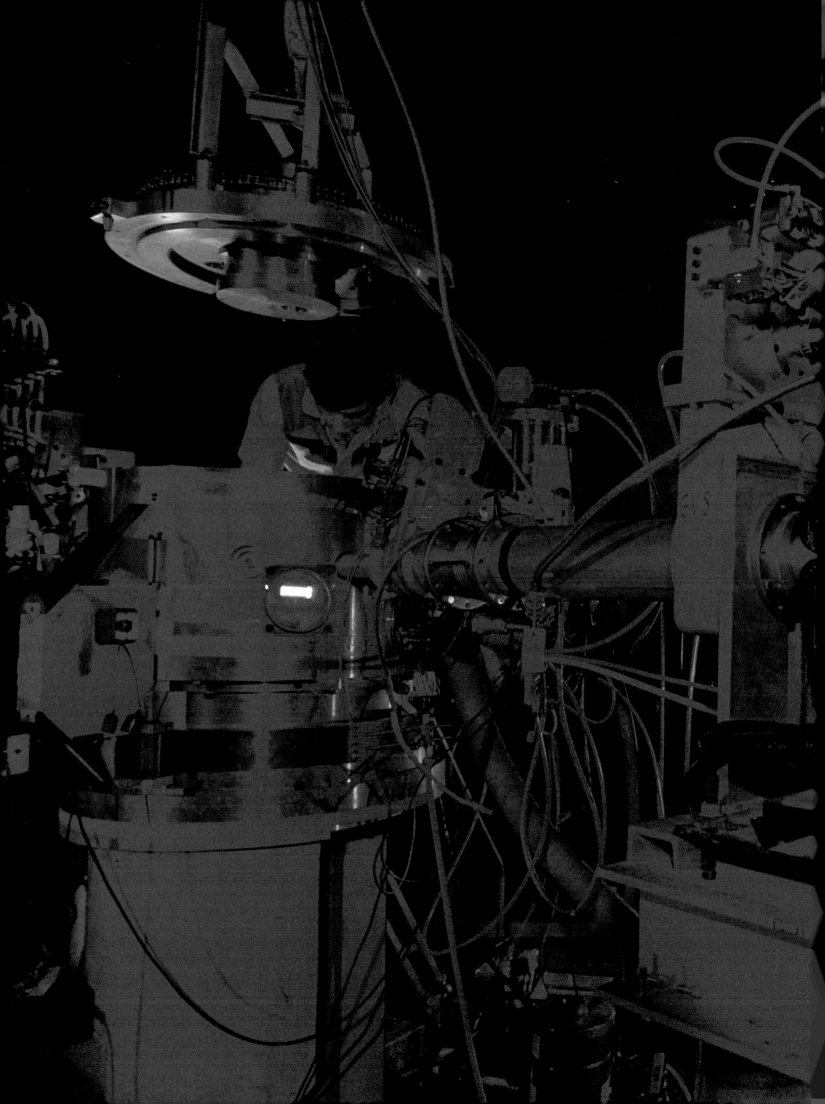

Maxwell Hall

29

Indiana Memorial Union

Indiana University has a lovely campus, with buildings all of Indiana limestone. We stayed in the Union Building, which is a memorial to the students of the University. Its memorial plaque reads "In memory of the sons and daughters of the University who have served in the war of the republic"....It is a delightful building.

Eleanor Roosevelt, in her newspaper column, 1950

I am very pleased to once again be incarcerated in that Gothic fortress you call the Union Building. It reminds me of a set from one of my old movies. And imagine my surprise when I looked out my window and saw that cozy little cemetery.

Vincent Price, lecture at IU, 1984

Beck Chapel

Beck Chapel, interior

Clock Tower, Student Building

I insist that the Hoosier is different mentally and spiritually to the average person. He is softer, less sophisticated, more poetic and romantic. He dreams a lot. He likes to play in simple ways. He is not as grasping as some other Americans. In a crude way, perhaps, he has the temperament of the artist, and so I still look to Indiana and its children, at least, to do great things artistically.

Theodore Dreiser, in *The Nation*

Overleaf: Musical Arts Center

Maybe the most powerful musical impression in my life was a visit to the Indiana School of Music at Bloomington. They have a theater there, and several university orchestras. They learn all the crafts of the theater — set design, direction, lighting, costuming — and they put on ballet and opera. It is very impressive.

Mstislav Rostropovich, in the *Washington Star*, 1978

IU Opera

The history of Indiana University has ever been prologue in the external effort to impart the timeliness of ancient ideals and dreams to succeeding generations of Hoosiers.

Thomas D. Clark, in *Indiana University (Vol. 1)*

IU Art Museum

There is an old Chinese proverb which says:
If you are planning for a year ahead, sow rice;
for ten years, plant trees; for a hundred years,
educate people.

Here in this irrefutable truth is reflected the
grave responsibility which our University has
for the shaping of the future of America and
the world. No small part of this responsibility
rests upon that division of the University, the
School of Business, which concerns itself with
the all-important element of management
skills — skills needed for every type of enterprise,
both public and private, that has to do with
the economic growth and vitality of our nation.

Herman B Wells, in *The First Half-Century:*
Continuity and Change, 1970

The School of Business

The University can put no bound to its interests narrower than those of the poet whose word has become a proverb quoted in the dictionaries: "I am a man, and nothing that belongs to a man is alien to me."

William Lowe Bryan , 1924

The Redsteppers

INDIANA

*I was a part of the University, and it was part of me.
It was so much a part of me that it was many years
after I left here before I could shake off the hold it had
on me and cease to think of her problems as my problems. I shall never cease to think of her nor cease to
love her. It is said that the things one remembers best
of his alma mater are not there at all. There are mem-
ories that cluster about the spirit of the place.*

Joseph Swain, in a speech, 1920

Read Hall

Wright Quad

East Lounge , Indiana Memorial Union

With such ample resources of land as we possess for building up and patronizing a great state institution of learning in Indiana, she should no longer indulge herself in a state of passivity on this subject, but at once admit the truism, that letters and intelligence are the precursors of power.

Gov. James Ray, speech to the Indiana General Assembly, December 8, 1826

Jordan Hall

Overleaf, pages 66-67: Chancellor Herman B Wells

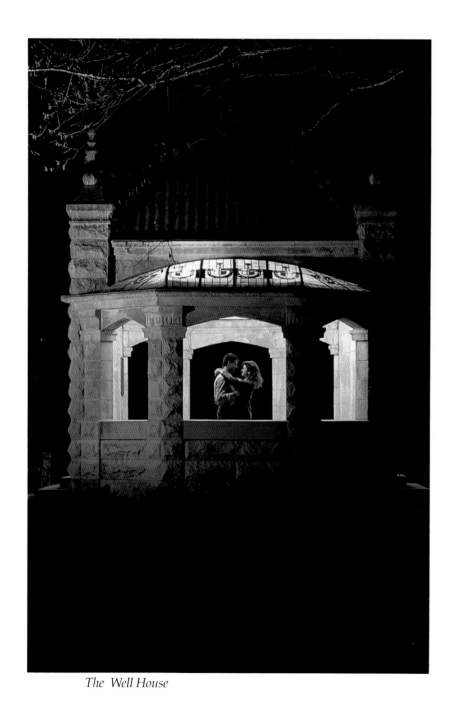

The Well House

IU Auditorium

Overleaf: Kirkwood Hall

The mission of a great university is the preservation, creation and communication of knowledge. If one contemplates that mission, it is obvious that central to the very heart of any university is its library. On the adequacy of that facility rests a university's reputation and the quality of her educational programs.

Joseph R. Hartley, Vice President and Dean of Academic Affairs, 1970

South Lounge, Indiana Memorial Union

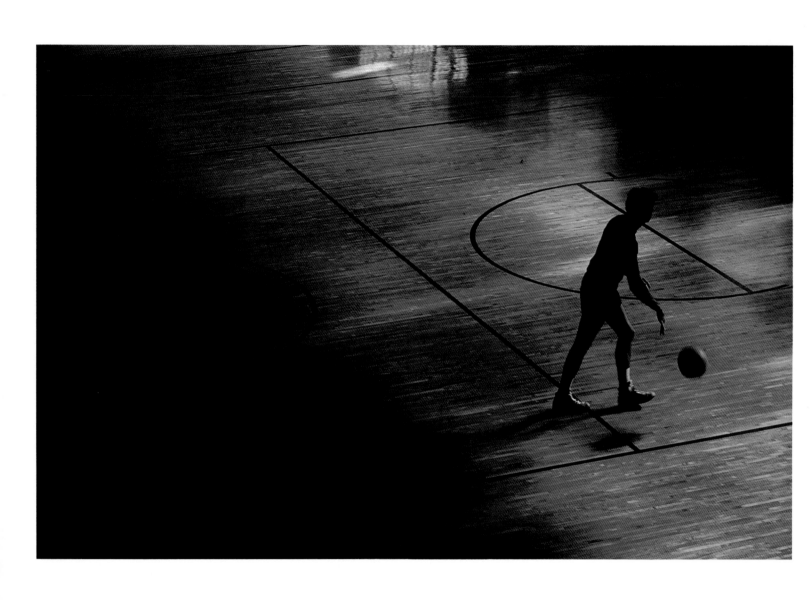

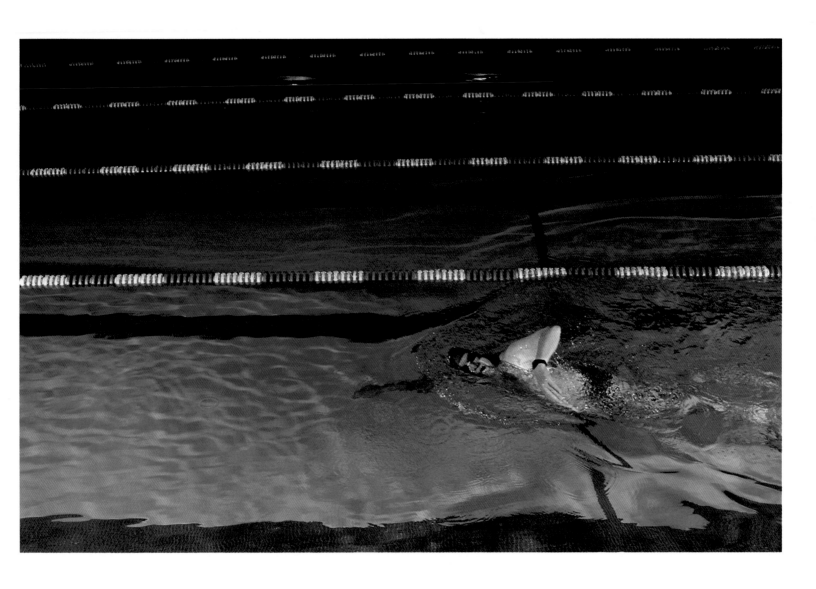

Assembly Hall

IU basketball coach, Bob Knight

Assembly Hall

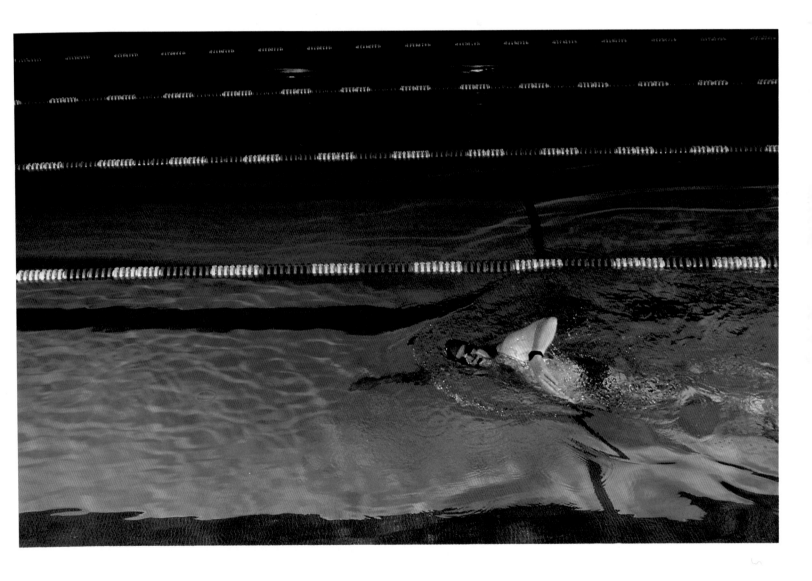

NCAA national championship basketball trophies: 1940, 1953, 1976, 1981

National champions, 1987

Madrigal dinner

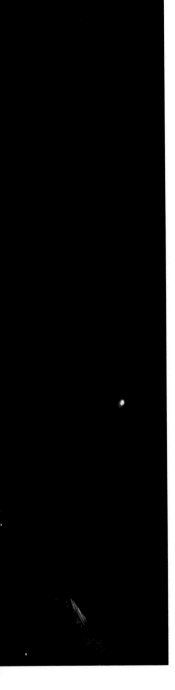

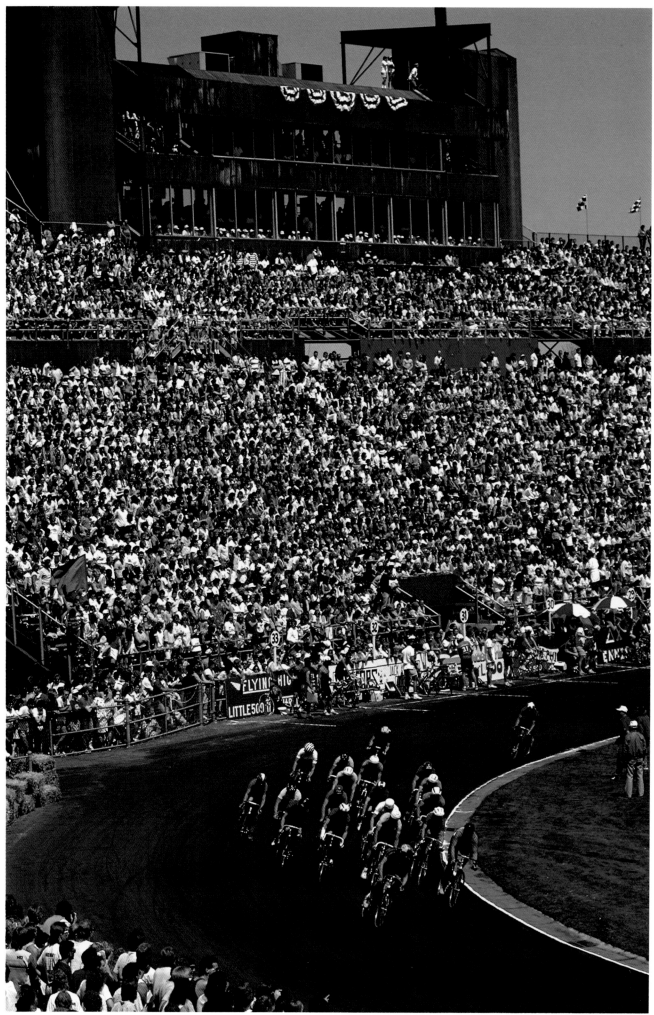

The Little 500

Monroe County Courthouse

One thing my mother never taught me: What is the true derivation of the word "Hoosier"? Perhaps nobody knows....At any rate, whatever may be its derivation or its meaning, I can claim a direct and indisputable link with the Hoosier tradition.

Rt. Hon. Harold MacMillan, 1956

Ballantine Hall

The Jordan River

I shall always keep in mind this scene here in the open by the University buildings, a University which, in what we are apt to think of as a new nation, is approaching its centenary, here under these great trees, these maples and beeches, that have survived over from the primeval forest....it is a sight I shall never forget — it will always be with me.

Theodore Roosevelt, IU Commencement, 1918

Gutenberg Bible, Lilly Library

Maxwell Hall

Commencement

My charge to you is to acknowledge the ambition which brought you here, energized you to respond to the years of academic challenge and which fires your zest for your career to come. Acknowledge that ambition — it is a worthy characteristic — and harness it; make yourselves ambitious for yourselves and success, also be ambitious for your generation and its progress and for your Alma Mater.

IU President John Ryan, Commencement, May 9, 1987

HAIL TO OLD IU

Come and join in song together,
Shout with might and main;
Our beloved Alma Mater,
Sound her praise again.

Honor to the Cream and Crimson,
Banner that we love;
It shall lead us in the conflict,
And our triumph prove.

Senior, Junior, Soph and Freshman,
All together we
Sound the chorus loud and glorious,
State University.

Here's to her whose name we'll ever
Cherish in our song;
Honor, love, and true devotion,
All to her belong.

Gloriana, Frangipana, E'er to her be true!
She's the pride of Indiana, Hail to old I.U!

J.T. Giles, BA, 1894